The Wildlife Trusts Guide to
# TREES

## Series Editor Nicholas Hammond

Illustrated by Cy Baker

NEW HOLLAND

First published in 2002 by
New Holland Publishers (UK) Ltd
London • Cape Town • Sydney • Auckland

10 9 8 7 6 5 4 3 2 1

Garfield House, 86-88 Edgware Road, London
W2 2EA, United Kingdom
Website: www.newhollandpublishers.com
80 McKenzie Street, Cape Town 8001, South Africa
Level 1/Unit 4, 14 Aquatic Drive, Frenchs Forest,
NSW 2086, Australia
218 Lake Road, Northcote, Auckland, New Zealand

ISBN 1 85974 965 8

Publishing Manager: Jo Hemmings
Project Editor: Mike Unwin/Camilla MacWhannell
Production: Joan Woodroffe

**Packaged by Wildlife Art Ltd:**
www.wildlife-art.co.uk
Design and Cover Design: Sarah Crouch
Art/Copy Editor: Sarah Whittley
Text: Sylvia Sullivan
Proof-reading and Index: Rachel Lockwood
**Illustrator: Cy Baker**

Reproduction by Modern Age
Repro Co. Ltd, Hong Kong
Printed and bound in Singapore by
Kyodo Printing Co (Singapore) Pte Ltd

# Contents

Since 1912, The Wildlife Trusts have been speaking out for wildlife and undertaking practical action at the local level throughout the UK. Believing that wildlife is essential to a healthy environment for all, The Wildlife Trusts work with people from all walks of life – communities, industry, government, landowners, and families – to make sure nature gets a chance amongst all of the pressures of the modern world.

With years of experience and the service of the UK's top naturalists, The Wildlife Trusts and Wildlife Watch – the UK's leading club for young environmentalists – play a key part in restoring the balance between new developments and the natural world. With the specialist skills of volunteers and staff they manage more than 2,300 wildlife reserves (totalling more than 80,000 hectares), which are among the finest sites in the UK.

Their members, who number more than 340,000, contribute to their achievements by their generosity and hard work, and by spreading the message to everyone that wildlife matters.

The Wildlife Trusts is a registered charity (number 207238). For membership, and other details, please phone The Wildlife Trusts on 0870 0367711 or log on to www.wildlifetrusts.org

**A**bout 11,000 years ago, the ice that once covered Europe began to retreat. A tundra landscape followed and with it the return of the trees that were forced southwards. The Irish Sea, English Channel, North Sea and Baltic did not exist and the trees movement northwards was steady, albeit slow. The first species to move north were birch, aspen and sallow. Other species followed. As climate stabilised about 8500 to 6000 years ago, some of the tree species became dominant.

The primeval forest that once covered much of Europe now survives in a very few places. The Bialowieza Forest in Poland is a good example. Most forests have been cleared and replanted. Man began clearances about 6000 years ago, creating a huge impact on the environment. Once our ancestors realised that trees produced a material that had uses other than firewood, they were ingenious in their production of useful crops. By coppicing and pollarding they both increased the lives of trees and produced wood of length and shape that was suitable for a variety of uses. Coppicing of hazel every five to six years, for example, produced rods of suitable width to be used as laths in wattle and daub walls of houses. Woodland management declined in the twentieth century, its revival over the last 25 years was in great part due to nature conservationists. They realised that traditional woodland management created the mixture of sizes and ages of trees that provided the conditions needed for the survival of dormice, butterflies, beetles and songbirds. The Wildlife Trusts across Britain have many woodland nature reserves and are leaders in the management of woodlands to produce the greatest quantity of wildlife.

In south-west Spain the *dehesa*, a wood-pasture, has been managed in the same way for at least 2000 years. This is an extensive farming system that depends on the delicate balance between trees, livestock and a rotational farming regime. The holm-oaks, are pruned to have three main branches with no crown, so that maximum sunlight reaches the forest floor, encouraging the growth of flowers. The flowers attract the bees which pollinate the trees thus providing acorns, on which the pigs feed. This is a sustainable farming system, albeit one that produces a standard of living for the farmer scarcely above subsistence.

The holm-oaks of the dehesa are much smaller than the same species planted as ornamental trees on the south coast of England. Many trees have been introduced for ornamental purposes, especially in cities and parks, while there have been several species of conifer introduced for commercial purposes. Many trees that are familiar are not indigenous to the country in which they are seen. Only 35 species are native to the British Isles, for example. In this book we give the areas from which each tree originates.

## What is a tree?

The definition of a tree is a woody, perennial plant that can reach more than six metres on a single stem. Since trees take many years to reach maturity, many may never reach the height of six metres because of human interference, such as coppicing and pollarding.

Like all organisms, plants have been divided into taxonomic groups; the most important of which are the class, the order, the family and the species. The family for each tree included in this book is given. In addition to the common English name there is the scientific name of the species. The scientific name contains two names: the first is the genus and is shared by several species, while the second is the specific name. Thus, the Scots pine is *Pinus sylvestris* while the black pine is *Pinus nigra*. However, there are two varieties of black pine, one from Corsica and one from the Pyrennees. They are described as *Pinus nigra var. pyrenaica* and *Pinus nigra var. maritima*. Geographically isolated populations of species may develop their own characteristics and eventually will become separate species and unable to breed with other geographically separate populations of the original species. Human interference has confused this by interbreeding different varieties and interbreeding can lead to difficulties with identification.

Hybrids may be between species, or between varieties of the same species in which case it may look sufficiently like either of its parents as to be indistinguishable. The third type of hybridism is inter-generic where trees of different genera interbreed. The less closely the two species are related the more vigorous the resulting hybrid will be. It will grow higher and probably bear more fruit. Hybrid vigour is beloved of plant breeders, an excellent example of this is the Leyland cypress, a tree considered by some to be a pest. This tree was bred from two North American species, the Monterey cypress *Cupressus macrocarpa* and the Nootka cypress *Chamaecyparis nootkatensis*. As a hybrid the Leyland cypress's scientific name is prefixed by a cross — thus, *x Cupressocyparis leylandii*. Unlike animals, hybrid plants can produce fertile offspring, although the hybrid vigour diminishes within a few generations.

## Flowers

Trees bear flowers, although in temperate Europe, where insects are a major means of pollination, they are smaller and less obvious than those in the tropics and sub-tropics, where birds and tree-climbing mammals have a role in pollination. A single flower may be male, or female, or both. It may be simple or complex, appearing in many forms such as the catkins of hazels and pea-blossom flowers of acacia. In some species, which are called *dioecious*, all the flowers of an individual tree are of one sex, while in other *monoecious* species such as conifers, there are male and female flowers on each tree.

## Identifying trees

Identifying trees is a deductive process based on single features or a combination of features. From the shape it may be possible to identify the genus. The leaves, flowers and bark may all be diagnostic. In woods it may not be possible to see the shape clearly and the leaves and bark become more important. In winter deciduous trees will not be in leaf, but the size, shape and structure of fallen leaves will still be an essential aid to identification.

Please remember that trees, perhaps more than any other organism, have been moved around the world by man and have been interbred. This may make identification difficult, but it does give us a chance to see many exotic species, without having to travel the four corners of the world.

## Atlas cedar
*Cedrus atlantica*

DESCRIPTION Height 20–35 m; bole to 1.5 m diameter. Evergreen, coniferous. Crown broadly conical at first, becoming wider with age. Bark is dark grey. Branches ascending. Leaves are needle-shaped, blue-green or dark green, growing singly on current year's shoot 1.5–2 cm.

FLOWERS/FRUIT Male flowers pinkish; female flowers green. Male and female cones open in autumn.

HABITAT Native to Atlas mountains. Now widespread as an ornamental on a variety of free-draining soils.

## Deodar cedar
*Cedrus deodora*

DESCRIPTION Height up to 40 m; bole up to 1.5 m diameter. Evergreen, coniferous. Distinguished from other cedars by conical shape, drooping branches and longer leaves. Bark is dark grey-brown. Needles are soft, 3.5–4.5 cm x 1–1.5 mm.

FLOWERS/FRUIT Male flowers are erect, releasing yellow pollen in autumn. Female flowers are green and ripe cones 8–13 cm are dark brown.

HABITAT Native to Himalayas. Widely planted as ornamental tree. Dry mountainous areas.

# Cedar of Lebanon
*Cedrus libani*

DESCRIPTION  Height 20–40 m; bole 1–2 m diameter. Evergreen, coniferous.
Tree is broadly rounded with flat top. Massive branches grow horizontally.
Bark is smooth, brown or dark grey at first, darkening with age and
becoming cracked. Leaves are dark green needles, 1–3 cm long.
FLOWERS/FRUIT  Male flowers release yellow pollen in autumn. Female
flowers are pale green. Cones 7–10 cm
long are erect and barrel shaped.
HABITAT  Native to Lebanon,
Syria and southern
Anatolia. Mountain
slopes. Now widespread
ornamental.

## Lawson cypress
*Chamaecyparis lawsonniana*
DESCRIPTION Height 20–40 m; bole up to 1.2 m diameter. Evergreen. Bark at first is cinnamon-red, turning rich dark brown. Leading shoot is drooping and small leaves are 3–8 mm.
FLOWERS/FRUIT Female flowers grow on ends of small branchlets. Male flowers grow on ends of branches and have black scales. Cones are spherical up to 8 mm across.
HABITAT Native to North America. Ridges and valley slopes in the wild. Tolerates a variety of soils. Widespread ornamental.

## Western red cedar
*Thuja plicata*
DESCRIPTION Height 25–45 m; bole up to 1.5 m diameter. Evergreen, fast-growing. Bark cinnamon-red, turning greyish. Leading shoot almost erect. Leaves 3 mm long, bright green on top, lower side paler, very fragrant.
FLOWERS/FRUIT Female and male flowers borne at the end of short branches. Male flowers reddish; female flowers yellowish-green. Leafy cones about 1 cm long mature in one year.
HABITAT Native to North America. Popular tree, also grown for forestry. Moist, acid soil and swamps in the wild.

# Western hemlock

*Tsuga heterophylla*

DESCRIPTION Height 40–50 m, bole up to 1.5 m diameter. Evergreen, coniferous. Leading shoot arches widely so tip points downwards, giving whole tree a drooping appearance. Young stems are hairy. Needles taper to a blunt tip, vary in length from less than 5 mm to about 18 mm. Grown commercially for paper pulp.

FLOWERS/FRUIT Flowers in late spring on last year's growth, male cones are red. Mature cones are 2–3 cm long, light brown with a few rounded scales.

HABITAT Native to Pacific seaboard of North America. Moist acid areas, lower slopes. Will grow in shade. Grown commercially for paper pulp. Brought to Britain during 19th century as decorative specimen.

### Juniper
*Juniperus communis*

DESCRIPTION  Small conical tree with height up to 6 m, or a low-growing twisted shrub with spreading branches. Bark is a rich reddish-brown. Leaves are short spreading needles, spiky blue-green, borne in whorls of three.

FLOWERS/FRUIT  Male and female flowers grow on separate plants. Male flowers are yellow, females green. Berries are green in first year, and ripen to dark purple in second.

HABITAT  A variety of soils, likes lime-rich. Scattered throughout Europe.

### Japanese larch
*Larix kaempferi*

DESCRIPTION  Height up to 30 m, bole up to 80 cm diameter. Deciduous, coniferous. Long, thick, horizontal branches, though can "corkscrew". Bark is similar to European larch but more orange. Needles are blue-green, singly on long shoots, clustered in rosettes on short shoots. Purple cast in autumn.

FLOWERS/FRUIT  Male flowers are yellow and globe-shaped, female flowers are greenish or pink. Cones are squat and rounded with scales, 2.5–3 x 2–2.5 cm.

HABITAT  Native to Japan. Widespread timber tree in north-west Europe.

## European larch
*Larix decidua*

DESCRIPTION  Height can
be over 40 m. Deciduous,
coniferous. On a mature
tree the lower stem is clear
of branches. Branches higher up
are sparse, thick and horizontal.
Needles are light green and soft.
On long shoots they grow singly, on
short shoots they are clustered in
rosettes. Bark is light brown.
FLOWERS/FRUIT  Female flowers are loganberry-red with green stripes.
Male flowers are yellow and globe-shaped. Egg-shaped cones 1.5 cm wide.
HABITAT  Native to Alps and Carpathians. Mountainous but now widely
planted for forestry and ornamental.

## European silver fir
*Abies alba*

DESCRIPTION Narrow, conical tree up to height of 46 m, bole up to 2 m diameter. Evergreen, coniferous. Crown is cone-shaped with regular whorls of horizontal branches, upturned near their ends. Bark is dark grey. Needles are shiny green on top and silvery beneath – up to 3.5 cm long.

FLOWERS/FRUIT Yellow male flowers are grouped on undersides of twigs. Green female flowers on upper sides near top of tree. Cones 10–15 cm long.

HABITAT Native of central European highlands. Prefers cool moist climate and acidic soil.

## Spanish fir
*Abies pinsapo*

DESCRIPTION Regular conical shape with dull green foliage. Height up to 25 m, bole up to 1 m diameter. Evergreen, coniferous. Leaves are arranged in almost perfect radial formation. The needles are short, prickly, 1–2 cm long perpendicular to stem, hence its other name, hedgehog fir.

FLOWERS/FRUIT Male and female flowers grow on same tree. Male flowers are large and cherry-red, females pale green. The cones are purplish-brown, 10–15 cm long, with concealed bract scales.

HABITAT Native to south-western Spain. Introduced elsewhere. Prefers rocky, chalky areas. Not very common.

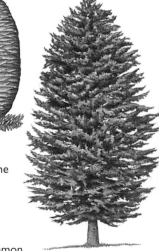

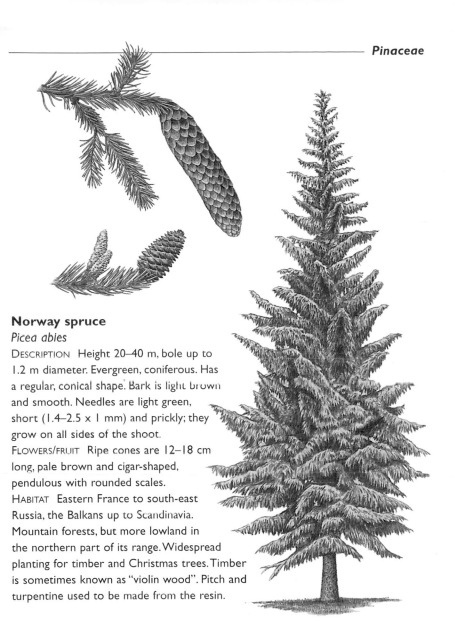

## Norway spruce
*Picea abies*

DESCRIPTION  Height 20–40 m, bole up to
1.2 m diameter. Evergreen, coniferous. Has
a regular, conical shape. Bark is light brown
and smooth. Needles are light green,
short (1.4–2.5 x 1 mm) and prickly; they
grow on all sides of the shoot.
FLOWERS/FRUIT  Ripe cones are 12–18 cm
long, pale brown and cigar-shaped,
pendulous with rounded scales.
HABITAT  Eastern France to south-east
Russia, the Balkans up to Scandinavia.
Mountain forests, but more lowland in
the northern part of its range. Widespread
planting for timber and Christmas trees. Timber
is sometimes known as "violin wood". Pitch and
turpentine used to be made from the resin.

## Sitka spruce
*Picea sitchensis*

DESCRIPTION Height 20–60 m, bole up to 3 m diameter. Evergreen, coniferous. Crown begins as narrow cone, then broader with long heavy branches. Needles are slender, flat and sharply pointed 1–2.5 cm long, blue-green above with two white bands beneath.

FLOWERS/FRUIT Male flowers are pale yellow; female flowers are greenish-red. Cones 5–10 cm long are light brown. Seeds have thin papery wings.

HABITAT Native to coastal west North America. Widely planted for timber throughout north-west Europe.

## White spruce
*Picea glauca*

DESCRIPTION Height 15–20 m, bole up to 50 cm diameter. Slow-growing evergreen tree. Crown is conical, but becomes more spire-like. Pink-grey bark at first becomes ash-brown. Tapered leaves, bluish-green with silver-white lines, 1–1.7 x 1 mm.

FLOWERS/FRUIT Flowers in spring on shoots of the previous season; male flowers are yellow. Fruit is a long brown cone, 2.5–6 x 1.5–2.5 cm.

HABITAT Native to North America. Grown throughout northern Europe for timber.

## Lodgepole pine
*Pinus contorta var. latifolia*
DESCRIPTION Height 20–25 m, bole up to 1 m
diameter. Evergreen. Crown is cone-shaped.
Bark is scaly, brown. Leaves are blue-
green tapered and usually twisted,
4–5 cm x 1–1.5 mm.
FLOWERS/FRUIT Flowers in late spring on
current season's growth. Male cones yellow.
Fruit takes two years to mature – brown
egg-shaped cone, 5 x 2.5 cm.
HABITAT Native to North America, coastal,
from south-east Alaska to California. Grown
in Europe for forestry and as an ornamental.

## Stone pine
*Pinus pinea*
DESCRIPTION Height 15–20 m, bole to 1 m
diameter. Evergreen. Crown is conical at first but
as tree ages branches radiate. Bark is orange, fissured,
developing deep furrows and scaly plates. Leaves are
grey-green in bundles of two, 8–18 cm x 1–2 mm.
FLOWERS/FRUIT Flowers in mid-summer on current
season's growth. Male cones orange-brown. Fruit takes
three years to mature – brown cone 8–15 x 6–10 cm.
Seeds are 2 cm long, edible.
HABITAT Mediterranean region. Sandy sites in warm
Europe as ornamental.

## Maritime pine
*Pinus pinaster*

DESCRIPTION Height 20–30 m, bole to 1.5 m diameter. Evergreen. Crown cone-shaped, becoming domed. Bark orange-brown at first, then dark purple or rust-brown with deep fissures. Grey-green needles in bundles of two, 7–11 cm x 0.6 mm.

FLOWERS/FRUIT Flowers in late spring on current season's growth. Male cones yellow-brown. Fruit matures in second autumn – a shiny, brown cone, 8–20 x 4–6 cm. Seeds 1 cm with wings.

HABITAT Native to Atlantic France to Portugal, Mediterranean to Greece and Morocco. Coastal sand dunes.

## Western yellow pine
*Pinus ponderosa*

DESCRIPTION Height 20–40 m, bole up to 1.5 m diameter. Evergreen. Crown cone-shaped. Bark purple-grey to dark brown; old trees have deep fissures. Grey-green leaves in bundles of three, 11–22 cm x 1.5 mm.

FLOWERS/FRUIT Flowers in early summer on current season's growth. Male cones cylindrical, purple. Fruit matures in second year to a purple-brown cone in autumn 6–16 x 3.5–5 cm.

HABITAT Native to North America. Open hillside. Cultivated in Europe as ornamental.

## Japanese white pine
*Pinus parviflora*

DESCRIPTION Height 20 m, bole 60 cm diameter. Evergreen. Crown is a broad cone-shape, becoming more rounded or flat-topped. Bark is smooth, purple-grey. Leaves mid-green, bundles of five, twisted, 2–6 cm x 11–1.5 mm.

FLOWERS/FRUIT Flowers in early summer on current season's growth. Female cones green or pink, the male cones pink-purple. Fruit matures in second autumn – a sticky, brown cone, 5–7 x 2.5–3 cm. Seeds 1–1.3 cm long.

HABITAT Native to Japan. Cultivated as ornamental in Europe. Temperate mixed forest.

## Corsican pine
*Pinus nigra*

DESCRIPTION Height to 40 m, bole to 1.3 m diameter. Evergreen. Crown cone-shaped at first, but becomes more like a column as branches spread. Needles grey-green, in bundles of two, 12–18 cm x 1.5 mm.

FLOWERS/FRUIT Flowers in early summer on current season's growth. Female flowers pink, male flowers yellow and purple. Fruit ripens in second autumn – yellow or grey-brown cone, 5–9 x 3.5 cm.

HABITAT Native to Sicily, Calabria and Corsica. Used for forestry in Britain.

## Weymouth pine
*Pinus strobus*

DESCRIPTION Height 15–25 m, bole up to 2 m diameter. Evergreen. Irregular, conical shape. Crown becomes domed with maturity. Bark is dark grey, smooth when young, rough with maturity. Leaves grow in bunches at first, spreading in second year, grey-green, 8–10 cm x 0.7 mm.

FLOWERS/FRUIT Flowers on current season's growth. Male flowers yellowish, female flowers pinkish situated at the end of shoots. Clusters of male cones appear at base of shoot. Slightly curved, 10–20 x 1.5–2 cm.

HABITAT Native to North America. Mixed forest, sandy soils.

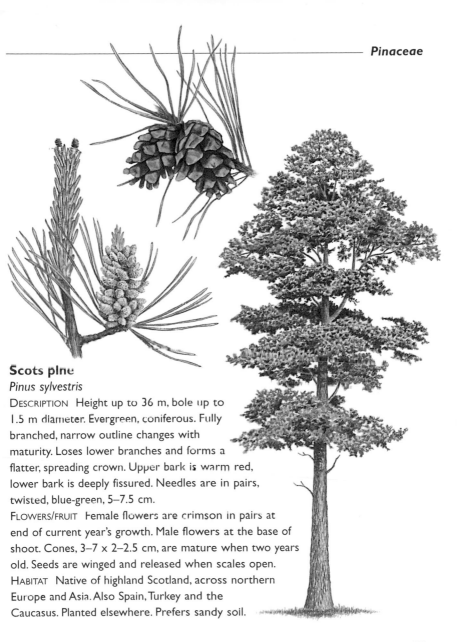

## Scots pine
*Pinus sylvestris*

DESCRIPTION Height up to 36 m, bole up to
1.5 m diameter. Evergreen, coniferous. Fully
branched, narrow outline changes with
maturity. Loses lower branches and forms a
flatter, spreading crown. Upper bark is warm red,
lower bark is deeply fissured. Needles are in pairs,
twisted, blue-green, 5–7.5 cm.

FLOWERS/FRUIT Female flowers are crimson in pairs at
end of current year's growth. Male flowers at the base of
shoot. Cones, 3–7 x 2–2.5 cm, are mature when two years
old. Seeds are winged and released when scales open.

HABITAT Native of highland Scotland, across northern
Europe and Asia. Also Spain, Turkey and the
Caucasus. Planted elsewhere. Prefers sandy soil.

## Aleppo pine
*Pinus halepensis*

DESCRIPTION  Height 20 m, bole up to 50 cm diameter. Evergreen, coniferous. Conical when young, maturing into rounded tree. Bark is silver-grey, maturing to red-brown with age. Needles in pairs, radial along shoot; they stay on tree for two years, 6–11 cm x 0.7 mm.

FLOWERS/FRUIT  Flowers on current season's growth, in early summer. Fruit matures in second autumn to a red-brown cone, 5–12 x 2.5–3.5 cm, but often stays on tree unopened for several years. Seeds have a wing 20 mm long.

HABITAT  Native to Mediterranean. Prefers, dry hillside country. Often planted as a wind-break.

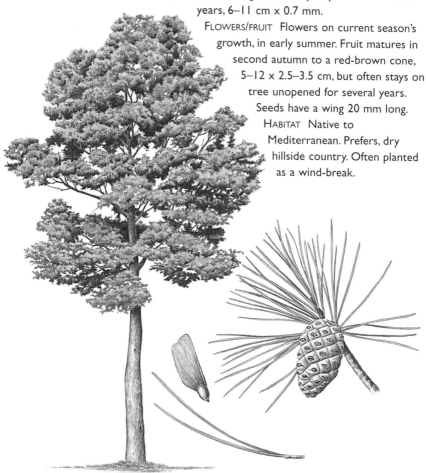

## Douglas fir
*Pseudotsuga menziesii*
DESCRIPTION  Tall, broadly conical tree, 25–60 m, bole up to 1 m diameter. Evergreen. Bark is dark grey. Needles are flat and grow all around the shoot, becoming dark glossy above, with two white bands beneath, 2–3 cm long.
FLOWERS/FRUIT  Male flowers are yellow, female flowers red, shaped like a tassel. Cones are pendulous, 7–10 cm long, light brown, with three pointed bract scales projecting.
HABITAT  Native to North America. Grown for timber in Europe. Prefers moist, acidic, sheltered conditions.

## Wellingtonia
*Sequoiadendron giganteum*
DESCRIPTION  Noted for its height, bulk and longevity. Can live up 1500 years, up to 3500 years disputed. Height 50 m, bole up to 3 m diameter. Evergreen. Bark is thick and fibrous. Leaves are scale-like, curve away from twig, 1 cm long with tip usually raised. Dark green, two bands of white dots underneath.
FLOWER/FRUIT  Male flowers pale yellow; female flowers green, on tips of shoots. Cones ripe in second year, 7 cm long.
HABITAT  Native only on Pacific slopes of Sierra Nevada, California. Planted elsewhere.

## California or Coast redwood
*Sequoia sempervirens*

DESCRIPTION Broadly columnar evergreen, reaching 15–50 m usually, but fast-growing and known to reach over 100 m. Bole to 2m diameter. Bark is thick and spongy, and scales off to reveal a red underbark. Young shoots are green and hairless. Leaves are two different kinds: on main branches they are scale-like all round the stem, 6–8 mm long. Those on smaller branchlets are linear and in two rows to left and right of stem. The needles are bright green above, and have two white bands underneath.

FLOWER/FRUIT Male flowers are yellow on tips of small shoots; female flowers green, 6 mm long. Egg-shaped cones grow on tips of larger shoots, 2–2.5 cm long.

HABITAT Native to Oregon and California in North America. Ornamental in Europe. Coastal, moist areas, in the wild.

## Dawn redwood

*Metasequoia glyptostroboides*

DESCRIPTION  Height 15–30 m, bole up
to 80 cm. Deciduous. Trunk is fluted
with shaggy reddish bark. Sparse
branches sweep upwards, producing
narrow conical tree. Leaves linear
and flat, 1.5–2.5 cm x 2–3 mm.

FLOWER/FRUIT  Flowers on shoots of the
previous year, in winter. Male cones are rare.
Female cones are egg-shaped, rather pointed,
ripening to brown in the first autumn. Buds are
unique, appearing below branches.

HABITAT  Discovered in 1941 in China, now grown in
Europe as an ornamental tree. Grows fastest in wet areas.

## Tulip tree

*Liviodendron tulipifera*

DESCRIPTION  Height 15–25 m, bole up
to 80 cm. Deciduous. Bark developes
rough ridges. Twigs have alternate
long-stalked hairless leaves, 7–12 cm
long, which develop into four lobes
with flattened tops.

FLOWER/FRUIT  Flowers open in June and July,
tulip-shaped, 4–5 cm high with three spreading
greenish-white sepals and six erect petals pale green
with broad orange band near base. Fruits form in
dense cone-like aggregate; fruit breaks into two dry,
long-winged seeds.

HABITAT  Native to North America. Ornamental tree elsewhere.

## Taxaceae

### Yew

*Taxus baccata*

DESCRIPTION Height 10–25 m, bole up to 3 m. Evergreen. Crown in young trees tends to be cone-shaped, becoming columnar, then domed. The bark is purple-brown, becoming scaly. Leaves are deep green with two paler bands on the underside, 2–3 cm x 3 mm. All parts of the tree, except for the red aril, are poisonous.

FLOWER/FRUIT Male and female flowers on separate plants. Flowers appear on shoots of the previous year, in late spring. Male cones in leaf axils. Fruit is a red aril, with a black seed, 1 cm x 6 mm.

HABITAT Throughout Europe, as far as North Africa. Grown in parks and gardens, occurs in woodland. Today clippings used for anti-cancer drugs. Traditionally used for English longbow.

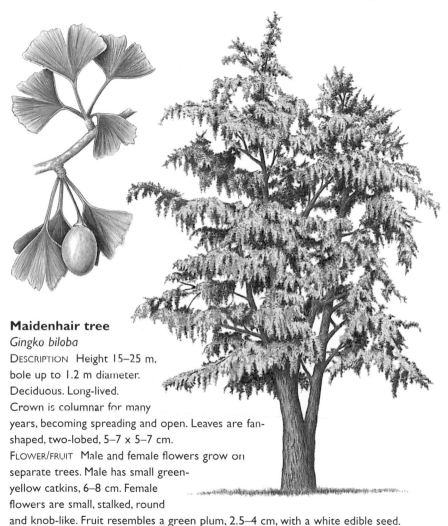

## Maidenhair tree
*Gingko biloba*

DESCRIPTION Height 15–25 m,
bole up to 1.2 m diameter.
Deciduous. Long-lived.
Crown is columnar for many
years, becoming spreading and open. Leaves are fan-
shaped, two-lobed, 5–7 x 5–7 cm.
FLOWER/FRUIT Male and female flowers grow on
separate trees. Male has small green-
yellow catkins, 6–8 cm. Female
flowers are small, stalked, round
and knob-like. Fruit resembles a green plum, 2.5–4 cm, with a white edible seed.
HABITAT Native to eastern China, grown widely for its seeds in eastern Asia.
Widespread in gardens as ornamental and in towns as amenity tree.

*Hamamelidaceae*

## Witch hazel
*Hamamelis virginiana*

DESCRIPTION Deciduous shrub or small tree. Height to about 5 m. Branches point upwards. Leaves are alternate with small teeth, unequal base and a long pointed tip, 10–15 cm, deep green and shiny upperside. They turn yellow in autumn.

FLOWER/FRUIT Flowers in autumn before leaves have fallen. Fruit is a 1 cm capsule enclosing two black seeds.

HABITAT Native to eastern North America. Grown in Europe as an ornamental and for its medicinal properties. Witch hazel is distilled from leaves and twigs to provide skin lotion.

# Bay laurel
*Laurus nobilis*

DESCRIPTION Also known as laurel,
poet's laurel and sweet bay. Vigorously
suckering shrub or small tree up to
20 m, bole to 60 cm diameter.
Evergreen, densely branched and
pyramidal in shape with dark blackish
bark. Hairless, lance-shaped leaves,
5–13 x 2–5 cm, with numerous oil glands. Strongly aromatic.
FLOWER/FRUIT Male and female flowers on separate trees. Female
flower has single ovary ripening to black single-seeded berry, 12 mm.
HABITAT Native to Mediterranean. Widely planted elsewhere.
Thickets and forest; planted in gardens where it is used in cooking.

## London plane
*Platanus x hispanica*

DESCRIPTION Height 20–40 m, bole up to 2 m diameter.
Hardy natural hybrid. Deciduous. Domed crown with
thick twisting branches. Bark is dark and
flakes in autumn, showing creamy
patches. Leaves alternate with five
lobes, 20 x 23 cm.

FLOWER/FRUIT Female flowers
are reddish, appearing at the
shoot tips. Male flowers are
yellow situated farther back
on stem. The bobble-like fruits
remain on the tree during winter.

HABITAT Origin unknown but
probably noted in continental
Europe. Widespread as an
ornamental tree, often lining
town avenues due to its
tolerance of pollution.

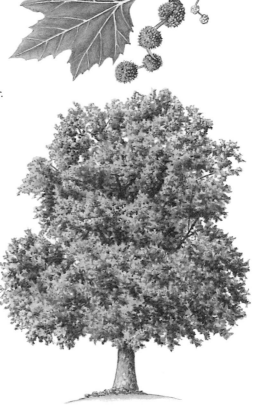

## Oriental plane
*Platanus orientalis*

DESCRIPTION Height 15–30 m, bole up to 3 m diameter. Deciduous, very long-lived hybrid. More rounded crown than London plane. Bark is pinkish-brown and flaky. Leaves have five to seven lobes, 9–20 x 9–20 cm.

FLOWER/FRUIT Female flowers reddish, appearing at the shoot tips. Male flowers are yellow situated farther back on stem. The bobble-like fruits remain on the tree during winter.

HABITAT Native of south-eastern Europe and Asia Minor. Near rivers and streams.

## Grey alder
*Alnus incana*

DESCRIPTION Height 20 m, bole up to 60 cm diameter. Deciduous. Smooth, grey-green bark, distinct pores. Leaves are alternate, pointed, elliptic, 5–10 x 4–6 cm. Upper surface is dull green, lower surface bluish-green and hairy.

FLOWER/FRUIT Separate male and female catkins on the same tree. Male catkins are long and drooping. Female catkins are short, egg-shaped, turning to green fruit, 1.5 cm long, remains on tree all winter, maturing in autumn.

HABITAT Northern and central Europe. Mountain valleys and sub-arctic forests.

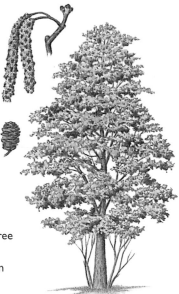

## Alder
*Alnus glutinosa*

DESCRIPTION

Height 15–25 m, bole up to 1 m diameter. Deciduous.

Conical shape with regular branches. Bark is rough and often sprouts shoots. Leaves are rounded and alternate, sometimes notched at the tip, 4–10 x 3–7 cm. Nodules on the roots contain nitrogen-fixing bacteria. The wood was used for clogs.

FLOWER/FRUIT Male and female catkins grow on the same tree. Buds are stacked with green fruits, ripening in spring. Female cones lengthen to 1–1.5 cm, becoming black and woody, staying on the tree all winter, opening to shed nutlets.

HABITAT Widespread throughout most of Europe. Thrives in wet ground, lining banks of rivers and streams.

# Silver birch
*Betula pendula*

DESCRIPTION Height 14–30 m, bole up to 40 cm diameter. Deciduous. Young bark is reddish maturing to black marked with silver-white. Slender habit with pendulous branches forming a pointed crown when young, domed when mature. Leaves are alternate on slender hairless stalks, triangular, pointed, margins with small teeth, 3–7 x 2.5–4.5 cm.

FLOWER/FRUIT Male and female flowers in separate drooping catkins on same tree in April and May. Inconspicuous and wind-pollinated. Fruiting catkins stay on tree until winter then break up into scaled and winged windborne seeds.

HABITAT One of Britain's native trees. Throughout Europe to northern Asia. Prefers light dry soils.

## Downy birch
### *Betula pubescens*
DESCRIPTION  Height 8–14 m, bole up to 80 cm diameter. Deciduous. Branches twisting, seldom hang down, and form a round-headed tree. Bark is red-brown. Leaves are rounded, hairy on underside, margin toothed, 1.5–5.5 x 1.5–4.5 cm.
FLOWER/FRUIT  Male and female flowers occur in separate catkins on same tree. Open in April; male catkin is pendulous, female is smaller and more erect. Fruit stays on tree in winter, breaking up into winged, windborne seeds.
HABITAT  Throughout Europe to central Asia. Moist areas and mountain forests.

## Himalayan birch
### *Betula utilis*
DESCRIPTION  Height 10–20 m, bole up to 60 cm diameter. Deciduous. Bark is red-brown and white. Pendulous branches forming a pointed crown when young, domed when mature. Leaves are egg-shaped, tapered, singly or in pairs on spur shoots, alternate on long shoots, toothed, 3–10 x 2–8 cm.
FLOWER/FRUIT  Male and female flowers on separate catkins on same tree in spring. Male catkins yellow and pendulous, female catkins erect. Fruiting catkins release winged seeds.
HABITAT  Himalayas to Tibet and west China. Widespread as ornamental.

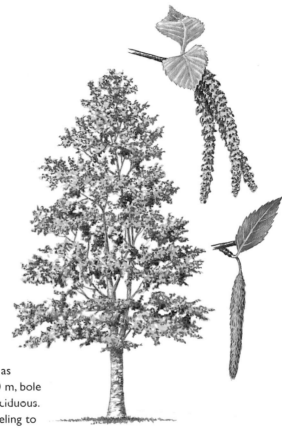

## Paper birch

*Betula papyrifera*

DESCRIPTION Also known as
canoe birch. Height 10–20 m, bole
up to 70 cm diameter. Deciduous.
Bark is a warm brown, peeling to
expose white underneath
continually renewed by further peeling. Leaves are egg-shaped, tapered to a point,
toothed, upperside matt green, light green and shiny below, 5–10 x 3–5 cm.
FLOWER/FRUIT Produces pendent yellow male catkins, and pendent cylindrical
fruits that release winged seeds.
HABITAT North America. Ornamental elsewhere. Grows in large forests in
moist sites in the wild. Bark was widely used to make canoes, baskets, and
covers for wigwams.

## Hornbeam
*Carpinus betulus*
DESCRIPTION  Height 15–25 m, bole up to 90 cm diameter. Deciduous. Rounded crown in mature trees. Bark is smooth, fluted in old trees, silver-grey colour. Leaves are broadly elliptical, acutely tapering, matt green toothed, 4–5 cm x 1–1.5 mm. Yellow and gold in autumn.
FLOWERS/FRUIT  Flowers in spring. Female flowers are green, male flowers drooping catkins, 3–5 cm long. Fruit is a leafy bract, set in pairs. Seeds are flat egg-shaped, 7 x 6 mm. Seeds are important food for birds.
HABITAT  Widespread across Europe to Asia Minor. Woodland, heavy soils.

## Hazel
*Corylus avellana*
DESCRIPTION  Height 8–10 m, bole up to 40 cm diameter. Deciduous. Rounded crown. Bark is light brown, becomes grey-brown in older trees. Leaves are rounded, heart-shaped at base, downy, serrated, 5–10 x 4–8 cm. Yellow in autumn.
FLOWERS/FRUIT  Flowers in late winter on previous season's growth. Female flowers from buds. Male catkins are yellow and pendulous. Fruit is a brown nut 1.5–2 cm long, with a leafy husk. Nuts are eaten by squirrels, voles and mice, also nuthatches and other birds.
HABITAT  Native to Britain and Europe. Woodland understorey. Grown for its nuts.

# Beech
*Fagus sylvatica*

DESCRIPTION Height 20–35 m, bole up to 1.8 m diameter. Deciduous. Domed crown, more conical in young trees. Bark is silver-grey, smooth. Leaves are oval, toothed, light green becoming darker, 6–10 x 4–7 cm. Yellow and brown in autumn.

FLOWERS/FRUIT Female flowers are green, male flowers globe-shaped on drooping stalks. Fruit is a small slightly prickly woody cup containing small nuts. Fruit is important food for birds such as tits and finches, as well as small mammals.

HABITAT Native to western and southern Europe, including southern England and south Sweden. Widely planted. Woodland on free-draining acidic and alkaline soils.

## Sweet chestnut
*Castanea sativa*

DESCRIPTION  Height 20–30 m, bole 2–3 m
diameter. Deciduous. Crown is conical in
young trees; older ones have broad
domed or spreading habit. Bark is grey, smooth at first, fissured later; often
spiralling up trunk. Leaves are lance-shaped, 15–20 x 7–10 cm. Yellow in autumn.
FLOWERS/FRUIT  Flowers in mid-summer. Male catkins erect, pale yellow,
becoming brown. Female flowers greenish. Fruit has large round prickly green
cases containing 1–3 nuts. Nuts are edible and good.
HABITAT  Native to Mediterranean region but widely planted. Prefers acidic soils.

## Turkey oak
### *Quercus cerris*

DESCRIPTION Height 20–40 m, bole 1–2 m diameter. Deciduous. Fast-growing oak. Crown cone-shaped at first, becoming rounded, then domed. Bark dull grey to silver-grey, fissured. Leaves oval with variable lobing, 5–14 x 3–6.5 cm. Brown in autumn.

FLOWERS/FRUIT Flowers in early summer. Inconspicuous female flowers. Male catkins drooping 5–6 cm long, crimson turning yellow-brown. Fruit is a plump acorn in scaly cup.

HABITAT Native to southern Europe. Woodland. Widely planted.

## Holm oak
### *Quercus ilex*

DESCRIPTION Height 30 m, bole 1–2 m diameter. One of the hardiest evergreens. Young trees grow like a column, crown becoming domed. Bark is brown-black, smooth at first then cracking into small squares. Leaves shed in the summer of their second year. Usually oval or lance-shaped, 4–8 x 2–3 cm.

FLOWERS/FRUIT Flowers in early summer; male catkins yellow, 4–7 cm. Acorn 1.5–2 cm in clusters of 1–3.

HABITAT Mediterranean. Prefers dry woods, coastal cliffs.

## Pyrenean oak
*Quercus pyrenaica*

DESCRIPTION Height 20–25 m, bole 80 cm diameter. Deciduous. Rather open crown is dome-shaped. Bark is light grey with deep fissures breaking into small square scales. Leaves are oval, broader towards the tip and lobed, 10–20 x 4–11 cm.

FLOWERS/FRUIT Flowers in late June with golden pendent male flowers. Acorn matures in one year; it is oblong and has a neat hemispherical cup holding the lower third.

HABITAT North-west France, Portugal, Spain and Morocco. Native to woodland.

## Sessile oak
*Quercus petraea*

DESCRIPTION Height 20–40 m, bole 2 m diameter. Deciduous. Taller than pedunculate oak, with which it hybridizes. Bark is grey-brown, smooth at first, later fissured and cracked. Leaves lobed, 8–14 x 4.5–8 cm.

FLOWERS/FRUIT Flowers in late spring; female flowers in groups of two to six towards tip of current season's shoots; male flowers pendent from buds on end of previous year's shoots, 5–8 cm. Acorns without stalks.

HABITAT Europe to 62°N; north-west Spain to northern Greece, across to western Poland. Prefers light acid soils.

## Pedunculate or English oak
*Quercus robur*
DESCRIPTION   Height 15–40 m, bole up to 0.7–3 m diameter. Deciduous. Young trees have cone-shaped crown, wide-domed in open situations. Bark is smooth and grey-green at first, then becomes fissured. Leaves with four to six lobes, 4–12 x 2–6 cm.
FLOWERS/FRUIT   Flowers in late spring; female flowers at end of new leaves, male catkins hang from buds. Acorns in clusters of one to four on slender stalks in shallow cups. Acorns eaten by jays, which are significant agents in dispersal.
HABITAT   Widespread throughout Europe. Woodland, hedgerows, open parkland. Supports hundreds of species of insects.

## Red oak
*Quercus rubra*

DESCRIPTION Height 20–35 m, bole up to 1.5 m diameter. Deciduous. Crown is cone-shaped, becoming wide-domed on radiating branches. Leaves have three to five pairs of large toothed lobes, 7–20 x 5–14 cm. Autumn colour is red, sometimes yellow or brown.

FLOWERS/FRUIT Flowers in May; female flowers in axils of new growth, male catkins. Acorns in broad shallow cup, 1.5–2.8 cm.

HABITAT Native to eastern North America, widely cultivated. Grown as ornamental tree and for forestry.

## Pin oak
*Quercus palustris*

DESCRIPTION Height 20–25 m, bole up to 1 m diameter. Deciduous. Crown is cone-shaped, slender at first, domed in old trees. Bark is smooth, dark silver-grey, fissured and darker later. Leaves are round or oval, with two or three pairs of lobes, 7–13 x 5–10 cm. Vivid red autumn colour.

FLOWERS/FRUIT Female flowers in axils of new growth in groups of three or four. Round acorns 1.2 cm, ripen in second autumn.

HABITAT Native to North America. Widely cultivated. Wet sites in the wild.

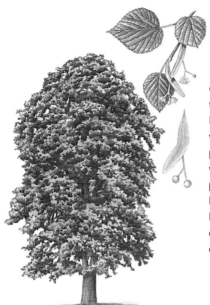

## Large-leafed lime
*Tilia platyphyllos*

DESCRIPTION Height 20–40 m, bole up to
1 m diameter. Deciduous. Young trees
have ascending branches and a narrow
crown. Leaves are heart-shaped, hairy and
toothed, 6–15 x 7–13 cm.

FLOWERS/FRUIT Flowers in mid-summer
with whitish-yellow, five-petalled, fragrant,
pendent flowers, which are attached to a
wing-like bract. Fruit is usually spherical,
pendent, about 1 cm.

HABITAT Native to Europe (including
England) through to Asia Minor. Widely
cultivated. Woodland. Also grown as
ornamental tree.

## Common lime
*Tilia europaea*

DESCRIPTION Height 20–45 m,
bole up to 2 m diameter.
Deciduous. Crown is a tall dome.
Bark smooth and dull grey becoming
brown and ridged, with much side growth.
Leaves are broader at base, to almost round,
toothed, often shiny and sticky with honeydew,
6–15 x 6–12 cm.

FLOWERS/FRUIT Highly scented flowers in July;
yellowish-white petals. Fruit is egg- or globe-
shaped, hairy, pointed tip, hanging in clusters 8 mm.

HABITAT European. Widely planted. Woodland.

## Small-leafed lime
*Tilia cordata*
DESCRIPTION Height 20–25 m,
bole up to 2m diameter.
Deciduous. Crown is a tall
rather narrow dome. The
branches ascend, but their tips
point downwards. Bark is smooth
and grey in young trees, old trees
have scaly bark near the base and
become dark grey or brown. Leaves
are rounded to egg-shaped, toothed, blue-green, 3–8 x 3–8 cm.
FLOWERS/FRUIT Flowers in mid-summer; with whitish-cream petals.
Fruit is globe-shaped or elliptical.
HABITAT Central Europe, including England, Norway and Sweden, to the
Caucasus. Woodland. Widely planted in towns and also used for forestry.

# Wych elm
*Ulmus glabra*

DESCRIPTION Height 20–30 m, bole up to 1m diameter. Deciduous. Crown in young trees is egg-shaped, becoming broadly domed. Bark is smooth, silver-grey, turning grey-brown and developing fissures. Leaves are in sprays, oval, 8–18 x 4–10 cm. Leaves turn yellow in autumn.

FLOWERS/FRUIT Red-purple flowers appear before leaves. Fruit is disc-shaped, with seed in centre surrounded by circular wing, hangs in bundles.

HABITAT Throughout Europe, not far north. Woodland and hedgerows.

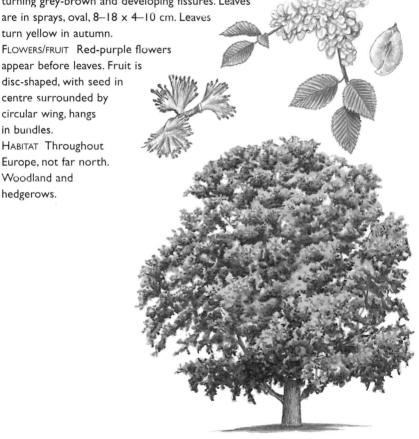

## English elm
*Ulmus procera*

DESCRIPTION Height up to 30 m, bole up to 1m diameter. Deciduous. Crown is egg- or cone-shaped at first, becoming a tall dome. Suckers grow from the roots. Leaves are rounded to oval, toothed, dark green, rough, 4–10 x 3.5–7 cm.

FLOWERS/FRUIT Flowers towards end of winter, early spring. Small red flowers are produced on last season's shoots. Fruit is disc-shaped with seed set in centre of circular wing, 1.2 cm.

HABITAT Southern England. Hedgerows, fields. Proliferated during enclosure, severely reduced in latter half of 20th century owing to Dutch elm disease – fungal growth spread by small beetle. Timber is valuable.

### Smooth-leafed elm
*Ulmus minor*

DESCRIPTION  Height 20–30 m, bole up to
1.2 m diameter. Deciduous. Crown is cone-
shaped, domed in older trees. Bark is smooth,
silver-grey, developing deep fissures. Leaves are
oval, base has one rounded side, one wedge-
shaped, toothed, shiny green, 6–8 x 2.5–5 cm.
FLOWERS/FRUIT  Purple-red flowers appear in early
spring on last season's growth. Fruit is a round
flat disc with seed in centre surrounded by a thin
wing, 1.2–1.5 cm.
HABITAT  Found in western Europe and North
Africa to south-west Asia. A tree of lowland
woodland.

### Fig
*Ficus carica*

DESCRIPTION  Height 10–15 m; bole up to 60 cm
diameter. Deciduous. Crown is low, broad and
spreading. Bark has fine wrinkles, pale-grey. Leaves
have three to five large rounded lobes, and are
dark green in colour, 30 x 35 cm.
FLOWERS/FRUIT  Flowers are pear-shaped, and
tiny, largely hidden within shoot tips. Pollination
is by insects. Fruit is green, maturing to purple,
pear-shaped with many seeds enclosed within
flesh, up to 5 cm.
HABITAT  Origins in western Asia, now
widespread in Mediterranean. Widely
grown for its delicious fruit.

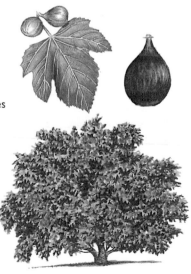

## Black mulberry
*Morus nigra*

DESCRIPTION Height to 10 m, bole up to 50 cm diameter. Deciduous. Crown is a low dome. Bark is orange-brown, brighter in the fissures. Leaves are broad, egg-shaped, wider towards the base, pointed tip, dull-green, rough, 8–12 x 6–8 cm.

FLOWERS/FRUIT Inconspicuous flowers in leaf axis appear in May. Fruit starts green, turning purple-black, 2–2.5 cm. Fruit is edible and good but usually used to flavour other fruit dishes.

HABITAT Widely cultivated. Origin uncertain. Grown as a fruit tree and as an ornamental.

# Tamarisk
*Tamarix gallica*

DESCRIPTION Height up to 8 m; bole up
to 20 cm diameter. Deciduous.
Crown is rounded. Bark is brown,
with fissures and scales. Leaves are
fine small, narrow, frond-like, give a
delicate, feathery appearance to
this small tree, 4 mm.

FLOWERS/FRUIT Flowers in summer
on short stalks carrying 5–10 cm racemes of
pink-white flowers. Fruit is a small capsule with
many seeds with hairs at one end.

HABITAT Coastal north-west France to North
Africa. Widespread as a small, garden tree and shrub.

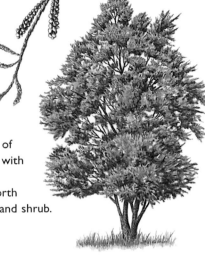

# Goat willow
*Salix caprea*

DESCRIPTION Height usually 8–12 m, but may be
up to 20 m, bole up to 1 m diameter.
Deciduous. Crown is domed. Bark is pale
grey, becoming orange within fissures,
smooth. Leaves egg-shaped, broader
towards base, dark to grey-green,
5–10 × 3–6 cm.

FLOWERS/FRUIT Flowers appear before
leaves in spring – female catkins green, male
catkins silver-grey tinged with yellow, 3 cm.
Fruit ripens in May/June, with many woolly seeds
on female catkins ("pussy willows"), 3–7 cm.

HABITAT European. Widespread. Wide range of soils.
Grown as a garden tree.

## Crack willow
*Salix fragilis*

DESCRIPTION Height 10–20 m, bole up to 1 m diameter. Deciduous. Crown is cone-shaped when young, becomes broad and rounded in mature trees. Bark starts off scaly, becomes deeply fissured, grey. Leaves lance-shaped, shiny green upperside, bluish-white underneath, 9–15 x 1.5–3 cm. Twigs root easily.

FLOWERS/FRUIT Flowers in April and May. Trees are either male or female. Male catkins are pale yellow, 4–6 cm long. Female catkins are green. White woolly seeds are formed on female catkin. Seeds are usually sterile.

HABITAT Central and southern Europe. Widely planted. Lowland, often on damp soil, near rivers.

## White willow
### *Salix alba*
DESCRIPTION Height 10–30 m, bole up to 1 m diameter. Deciduous. Mature crown is domed, with ascending branches. Bark shows deep fissures and is grey-brown. Leaves are lance-shaped, shiny with hairs, grey-green upperside, almost white underside, 5–10 x 0.5–1.5 cm.

FLOWERS/FRUIT Flowers in April. Male and female trees are separate. Pale yellow catkins; female catkins 3–4 cm, male catkins 4–5 cm. Fluffy seeds are formed on female catkins, ripen in July.

HABITAT Europe to central Asia. Near rivers, lowland.

## Grey willow
### *Salix cinerea*
DESCRIPTION Height 5–15 m, bole up to 30 cm diameter. Deciduous. Crown is egg-shaped. May grow on several stems. Bark starts off smooth, greyish brown, turning brown with fissures. Leaves oval to lance-shaped, upperside hairy at first, dark shiny green, grey-blue underneath, 2–9 x 1–3 cm.

FLOWERS/FRUIT Flowers in early spring, before leaves appear. Female catkins green, male catkins pale yellow, 2–3 cm. Fruit capsules contain silky seeds, 1 cm x 2.5 mm.

HABITAT Western Europe. Damp areas, hedgerows.

## Weeping willow
*Salix x sepulchralis*

DESCRIPTION Height 10–18 m, bole up to 1.3 m diameter. Deciduous. Crown is rounded, branches grow downwards. Bark is golden green when young, smooth; it becomes grey-brown and develops deep fissures. Leaves are lance-shaped, tapered upper surface has white hairs at first, underside is blue-green, 7–13 x 0.7–2 cm.

FLOWERS/FRUIT Flowers in spring on short leafy shoots. Usually male catkins appear, some female.

HABITAT This is a widely cultivated hybrid between *Salix alba* and *S. babylonica*. Associated with water and large gardens.

## Dwarf willow

*Salix herbacea*

DESCRIPTION  Small, low, prostrate shrub, branches 2 3 cm. Leaves shiny green, 6–10 mm long.

FLOWER/FRUIT  Produces green and yellow catkins.

HABITAT  Arctic and sub-arctic Europe, through to Pyrenees, central Apennines and Bulgaria. Rocky moorland over 600 m.

## Common osier

*Salix viminalis*

DESCRIPTION  Height 10 m. Deciduous. Has a narrow upright crown and grey bark with fissures. The leaves are narrow, lance-shaped and tapering, with dull green uppersides and silver-grey underside, 10–25 x 0.5–2.5 cm.

FLOWERS/FRUIT  Flowers appear before the leaves. Catkins are erect. Male flowers have yellow anthers. Fruit is flask-shaped. Male and female grow on separate twigs

HABITAT  Native to central and eastern Europe. Found in Britain. Prefers damp places. Cultivated for basket-weaving.

## Grey poplar
*Populus x canescens*

DESCRIPTION Height 25–40 m. Bole up to 2 m diameter. Deciduous. Crown is columnar, and open. Young bark is pale, whitish; lower trunk is black. Leaves are placed alternately and vary considerably in shape, white underside. Suckers readily from roots.

FLOWERS/FRUIT Male catkins are green; female catkins have a golden tinge. They grow on separate trees.

HABITAT Central Europe. Damp ground, near rivers and in water meadows.

## Black poplar
*Populus nigra*

DESCRIPTION Height usually 15–25 m, sometimes up to 40 m. Bole up to 1 m diameter. Deciduous. The crown is a large dome with spreading branches. Bark is grey-brown, with fissures and sometimes with burrs. Leaves are oval, with long pointed tip, about 8 cm long.

FLOWERS/FRUIT Male red and female green catkins form on separate trees. Fluffy seeds disperse in June.

HABITAT Probably native to Britain. Widely planted as a windbreak, beside roads, flourishes by water.

## White poplar
*Populus alba*

DESCRIPTION Height up to
25 m. Bole up to 1 m diameter. Deciduous. Crown is
columnar, open, with twisting branches. Bark is grey-white on upper tree.
Leaves have five small pointed lobes, tip is pointed, white underneath, 6–12 cm.
FLOWERS/FRUIT Male and female flowers appear on separate trees, before leaves
emerge. Female has green flowers; the male flowers are red. Fruit consists
of fluffy seeds.
HABITAT Western Europe to central Asia. Wet areas. Will grow near roads
and on sea coast. Slower-growing than black poplar.

## Aspen
*Populus tremula*
DESCRIPTION Height 15–25 m; bole up to 1 m diameter. Deciduous. Crown is cone- or column-shaped. Bark is green-grey, smooth. Leaves are round to oval, with sharp tip, toothed, upperside copper-coloured at first, becoming blue-green, yellow in autumn, 1.5–8 cm long. Leaves rustle in the lightest wind.
FLOWERS/FRUIT Male and female flowers on separate plants. Male are egg-shaped, green and brown; female are green. Seeds in 4 cm catkins in May.
HABITAT Europe to Asia Minor and central Asia. Damp hillsides and woods.

## Rhododendron
*Rhododendron ponticum*
DESCRIPTION Height 10 m. Evergreen. Usually on several stems to 15 cm diameter, combining to give spreading crown. Bark is brown. Leaves are lance-shaped, shiny dark green, 10–20 x 2.5–6.5 cm.
FLOWERS/FRUIT Flowers in late spring, early summer, with large blossoms of light purple to pink-purple. Fruit is a woody capsule, 2.5 cm.
HABITAT Native to Asia and possibly parts of Europe. Widespread. Difficult to eradicate, will smother other plants. Hillsides, and shaded woodland.

## Strawberry tree
*Arbutus unedo*

DESCRIPTION  Height 8–13 m; bole up to 1–2 m diameter. Evergreen. Trunk is short, often leaning, with a domed crown. Bark is dark red, shredding as tree ages. Leaves are elliptic or egg-shaped, wider near the tip, dark green, leathery, toothed, 5–10 x 1.5–4 cm.

FLOWERS/FRUIT  Flowers in October to December with drooping clusters of 15–20 white or pinkish flowers. The edible, but not very tasty, fruits mature through green and yellow to bright red, globe-shaped, 1.5–2 cm. They ripen in autumn as the flowers are opening.

HABITAT  Patchy distribution throughout southern Europe, to Cyprus, Turkey and western Ireland. Will tolerate damp acid soils to chalky hillsides. Planted as an ornamental tree.

## Wild pear
*Pyrus pyraster*

DESCRIPTION Height 12–25 m; bole up to 1.3 m diameter. Deciduous. Young trees have cone-shaped crown, domed in older trees. Bark is brown to blackish, with small, square plates. Leaves are rounded, with a short pointed tip, leathery, shiny green upperside, 2–3 x 3–4 cm. Leaves flutter and rustle in the lightest wind.

FLOWERS/FRUIT Flowers appear before leaves; white clusters, outer flowers open first. Fruit up to 6 cm, edible.

HABITAT A common wild European pear. Often confused with *P. communis*. Hedgerows and woods.

## Apple
*Malus domestica*

DESCRIPTION Height 8–12 m; bole up to 50 cm diameter. Deciduous. Crown is dome-shaped or rounded. Bark is grey-brown, smooth. Leaves are oval, slightly wider towards the base, toothed, dull green, 4.5–13 x 3–7 cm.

FLOWERS/FRUIT Flowers in April and May in clusters of four to seven flowers, pinkish or white. Fruit is the well-known apple, 5–10 cm, green, russet or red in colour, depending on variety.

HABITAT Widespread in temperate regions as a cultivated tree for its fruit.

## Crab apple
*Malus sylvestris*

DESCRIPTION Height 2–9 m; bole up to 40 cm diameter. Deciduous. Crown is rounded, with dense branches that curve downwards. Bark is dark brown, with fissures and cracks. Leaves are oval to egg-shaped, wider near the tip, serrated edge, 3–7 x 2–4 cm long.

FLOWERS/FRUIT Flowers have white or pink petals. Fruit is globe-shaped, like small apple, greenish. Edible but sour and is usually used to make jelly.

HABITAT Native to Europe. Widespread. Old woodland and hedgerows.
This tree is probably the ancestor of the cultivated apple.

## Medlar
### *Mespilus germanica*

DESCRIPTION Height 5–7 m; bole up to 60 cm diameter. Deciduous. Low crown, spreading branches. Bark is grey-brown, with fissures and oblong plates. Leaves are lance-shaped or oval, with dark yellow-green uppersides, 5–15 cm, tiny teeth round margin.

FLOWERS/FRUIT Flowers in May and June. White flowers occur singly on terminal shoots. Fruit is pear-shaped and edible, but not usually picked until after it has been frosted, 2–3 cm.

HABITAT Native to south-east Europe to Iran. Naturalised in central Europe. Woodland.

## Mountain ash or Rowan
### *Sorbus aucuparia*

DESCRIPTION Height 5–20 m, bole up to 30–60 cm diameter. Deciduous. Young trees have cone-shaped crown, older trees rounded or spreading. Bark is smooth, shiny, grey. Older trees are grey-brown with ridges. Leaves are pinnate with approximately 13–15 leaflets, 20 x 12 cm. May turn bright yellow or red in autumn.

FLOWERS/FRUIT Flowers in late spring with large clusters of creamy-white flowers. Fruits are red berries, usually ripened by August, liked by birds.

HABITAT Europe, the Caucasus and North Africa. Planted as ornamental.

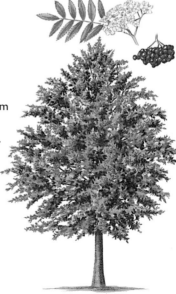

# Whitebeam

*Sorbus aria*

DESCRIPTION Height 15–25 m; bole up to 80 cm diameter. Deciduous. Young trees have cone-shaped crown that becomes domed in older trees. Bark is grey, smooth at first, turning scaly and fissured. Leaves are egg-shaped, margin serrated, 6–12 x 3–8 cm, with white underside.

FLOWERS/FRUIT Dull white flowers in clusters appear in May to June. Fruits are globe-shaped, bright red, in hanging clusters.

HABITAT Found naturalized; it occurs in southern England through southern Germany, Italy, Spain, Morocco and the northern Balkans. Prefers limey or chalky soils, but tolerates sandy conditions. Well drained, open woodland.

## Wild service tree
*Sorbus torminalis*

DESCRIPTION Height 15–25 m, bole up to 1.3 m diameter. Deciduous. Young trees have cone-shaped crown that becomes columnar and domed. May produce suckers. Bark is dark brown and grey, smooth, fissures and plates in old trees. Leaves have wide basal lobes, bronze, yellow and russet in autumn, 6–14 x 6–14 cm.

FLOWERS/FRUIT Flowers in June with clusters of white flowers. Fruit is globe-shaped, brown when ripe, in hanging clusters, 1–1.5 cm.

HABITAT Found in southern and central Europe, to Asia Minor and North Africa. Occurs in mixed woodlands.

## Wild cotoneaster
*Cotoneaster integerrimus*

DESCRIPTION Deciduous shrub whose height rarely exceeds 1 m. Twigs are hairless and do not carry thorns or spines.
Leaves are oval, untoothed, grey and woolly underneath, 15–40 mm long.

FLOWERS/FRUIT Small pink flowers in small clusters of two to four, 3 mm. Fruits are red berries, 6 mm. They are eaten by birds in autumn.

HABITAT Native to northern central Europe, including Britain, although rare. Prefers limestone.

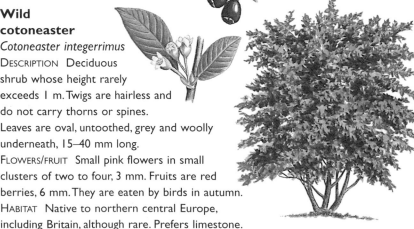

## Hawthorn
*Crataegus monogyna*
DESCRIPTION Also known as may or quickthorn. Height 10–16 m, bole up to 1 m diameter. Deciduous. Crown is rounded. Branches are dense, twigs bear sharp thorns. Leaves have two or three pairs of lobes, 1.5–5 x 2–5 cm, shiny green turning yellow or red in autumn. Supports many insects.

FLOWERS/FRUIT Flowers in May, in clusters of creamy-white flowers. Fruit is a small dark red berry, 8–14 mm, each containing one seed. Valuable food for birds, especially for thrush family.

HABITAT Widespread throughout all of Europe. Widely used as a hedging shrub. Also as a standard in woodlands.

## Midland hawthorn
*Crataegus laevigata*
DESCRIPTION Height 12 m, bole up to 60 cm diameter. Deciduous. Rounded crown, branches dense. Bark is grey- pink- or orange-brown, fissured and cracked. Leaves have one or two pairs of shallow lobes, upperside shiny green, yellow in autumn, 1.5–6 x 2–5 cm.

FLOWERS/FRUIT Flowers in May, in clusters of white or pink flowers. Bunches of red berries are produced, 8 x 11 mm, containing two or three seeds.

HABITAT Native to central and western Europe. Heavy soil, woodland. Hybrids planted as street trees throughout Europe.

## Blackthorn or Sloe
*Prunus spinosa*

DESCRIPTION  Height up to 5 m. Deciduous. Rounded crown, suckers readily, forming scrub. Twigs have sharp thorns. Bark is black and rough. Leaves are dull yellow-green, elliptic, 2–4.5 x 1.2–2 cm.

FLOWERS/FRUIT  White flowers appear in March to April, on the previous year's growth, before the leaves emerge. Fruit is globe-shaped, dark blue to nearly black, with a fleshy outer covering concealing a large stone 1.2 cm. The berry is eaten by birds and is also picked to flavour gin.

HABITAT  Native to Britain and Europe, except extreme north. A shrub of hedgerows and copse.

# Wild plum
## *Prunus domestica*
DESCRIPTION  Height 6–10 m; bole up to 30 cm diameter Deciduous tree with rounded crown; suckers readily. Bark is brown or grey-brown, becoming fissured. Leaves egg-shaped, wider towards the tip, 3–8 x 1.5–5 cm.

FLOWERS/FRUIT  Flowers in early spring, on previous year's growth, before leaves emerge. White flowers are single or in pairs. The fruit is globe-shaped, dark blue-purple when ripe, a large stone surrounded by juicy sweet flesh, 2–8 cm. Edible and good.

HABITAT  Native to Caucasus, but extensively cultivated. Orchards and gardens, but naturalized elsewhere.

# Cherry or Myrobalan plum
## *Prunus cerasifera*
DESCRIPTION  Height 8–12 m; bole up to 60 cm diameter. Deciduous. Young trees have upright crown that grows rounded and domed. Suckers grow from the roots. Bark is smooth, turning darker and with plates. Leaves are oval, toothed, deep shiny green above, matt green below, 4–6 x 2.5–3 cm.

FLOWERS/FRUIT  Flowers on previous year's growth in winter or early spring. Flowers are white. Edible fruit is red or purple when ripe, 2.5–3 cm.

HABITAT  Native to Balkans to central Asia. Hedgerows and field margins.

## Rosaceae

### Almond
*Prunus dulcis*

DESCRIPTION  Height 10 m; bole up to 30 cm diameter. Deciduous tree with a broad crown. Smooth bark, growing fissured, dark brown. Leaves are lance-shaped, with a pointed tip, dark to yellow-green, 4–12 x 1.2–3 cm.

FLOWERS/FRUIT  Flowers in late winter or early spring, on last year's growth. Large, showy, bright pink or pinkish-white flowers, 2.5–5 cm. Fruit is egg-shaped with a green fleshy rather felt-like skin that splits to reveal the nut, 3.5–6 cm.

HABITAT  South-west Europe, and North Africa. Prefers dry hillsides. It is widely cultivated for nuts, and ornamental.

### Wild cherry
*Prunus avium*

DESCRIPTION  Height up to 25 m; bole up to 1.5 m diameter. Deciduous. Crown is cone-shaped at first, then rounded. Bark is grey-pink to red. Young trees have shiny bark, which later becomes fluted with dark fissures. Leaves oval, margin serrated, dark green upperside, paler below and downy in young leaves, 7–12 x 4–5 cm.

FLOWERS/FRUIT  Flowers in April, in clusters with new leaves. The fruit is globe-shaped, dark red or yellow-red, 2 cm, enclosing stone.

HABITAT  Widespread through Europe. Also in North Africa, south-west Asia. Found in mixed woodlands.

## Bird cherry
*Prunus padus*

DESCRIPTION Height 10–20 m; bole up to 80 cm diameter. Young trees have cone-shaped crown, which tends to become domed. Branches droop. Bark is smooth, grey-brown. Leaves are elliptic or egg-shaped, wider towards the tip, margin serrated, 7–13 x 4–7 cm. Dark green, turning yellow and red in autumn.

FLOWERS/FRUIT Flowers in late spring, on side shoots. Flowers are white, produced on drooping racemes. Fruit is black, globe-shaped, up to 8 mm.

HABITAT North Europe to north Asia. Absent in Mediterranean. Temperate woodlands, preferring lime soils.

## Cherry laurel
*Prunus laurocerasus*

DESCRIPTION Height up to 15 m; bole up to 60 cm diameter. Evergreen. Crown is domed and rounded, often spreading with many different stems. Bark is black or grey-brown. Leaves are large, lance-shaped, in sprays, 8–20 x 3–8 cm.

FLOWERS/FRUIT Thirty to forty cream-coloured flowers are produced on erect racemes, in late winter on last year's growth. Globe-shaped fruit ripens in autumn to dark purple.

HABITAT Eastern Europe. Widely grown as an ornamental shrub. Understorey of woodland.

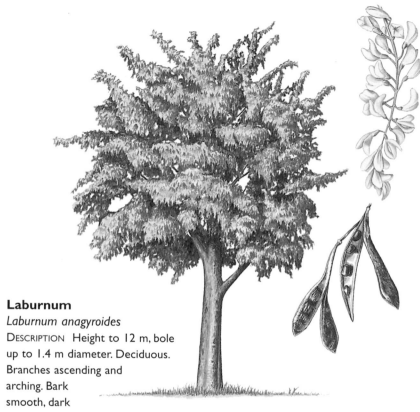

## Laburnum

*Laburnum anagyroides*

DESCRIPTION Height to 12 m, bole up to 1.4 m diameter. Deciduous. Branches ascending and arching. Bark smooth, dark green at first, then brown. Leaves are alternate; each leaf consists of three leaflets, 3–8 cm, rounded at the end but usually with sharply pointed tip. Grey-green on upper surface, silky white hairs, below. This tree is poisonous.

FLOWERS/FRUIT Yellow flowers are pea-like and poisonous, produced in May and June, hanging in long chains 10–30 cm. Pods, containing black seed, hang on tree in winter, 4–6 cm.

HABITAT Southern and central Europe. Popular small ornamental tree. Hybridizes with scottish laburnum, *L. albinum*. Scrub and woodland. The heartwood, which is very hard, has been used as a substitute for ebony.

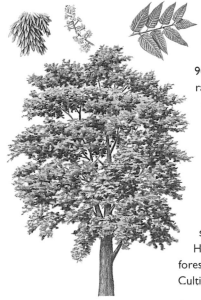

## Tree of heaven
*Ailanthus altissima*

DESCRIPTION Height 15–30 m, bole up to 90 cm diameter. Deciduous. Branches are radiating, giving rounded crown often with suckers. Bark smooth or scaly, grey-brown, with pale stripes. Leaves have unpleasant smell, are alternate, 13–23 red-stalked opposite leaflets, 60 cm. Deep green on top, pale and hairless beneath.

FLOWERS/FRUIT Male and female flowers open in May, usually grow on separate trees. Fruits in late summer, producing winged seeds, 3.5–4 x 1.2 cm.

HABITAT Native to northern China. Occurs in forests in the wild. May be planted in cities. Cultivated elsewhere.

## Judas tree
*Cereis siliquastrum*

DESCRIPTION Height 10–15 m, bole up to 60 cm diameter. Deciduous. Branches are spreading. Bark grey-brown, smooth or folded, becoming cracked. Leaves are alternate, with heart-shaped base, in two rows, 8–12 cm, wavy untoothed margin.

FLOWERS/FRUIT Flowers on short stalks, singly or in cluster, in May before or with leaves. Flat pods ripen to purple in autumn and remain on tree until well into winter, 10 cm.

HABITAT Native to Mediterranean and southern Europe to western Asia. Planted as ornamental. Hillsides in dry open areas.

## Bog myrtle
*Myrica gale*

DESCRIPTION Deciduous shrub growing to a height of about 2 m. Leaves are narrow, tapered towards base, wider towards tip, grey-green and fragrant, 2–6 cm.

FLOWERS/FRUIT Carries male and female catkins on separate plants. Male catkins are red-brown, 7–15 mm; female catkins are dark green, 4–5 mm. Fruit forms as small nutlets with wings, 5–10 mm.

HABITAT Western and northern Europe, including British Isles. Found in wet heath, lowland bog and fen.

## Silver gum
*Eucalyptus cordata*

DESCRIPTION Elegant evergreen, grown as a tree or a pruned shrub. It can also be coppiced. Bark is smooth, greenish-white and blotched. The leaves are heart-shaped, bluish-white, glaucous.

FLOWERS/FRUIT Flowers are fragrant, large and white. Large fruit.

HABITAT Native to Australia. Elsewhere grown as an ornamental. Grows best in fertile acid to neutral soils. Grown for timber. A comparatively tender tree that will not withstand hard frost. Foliage is valued by florists.

## Mountain gum
*Eucalyptus dalrympleana*
DESCRIPTION  Also known as
broad-leafed kindling gum. Height
20–35 m; bole up to 1 m diameter.
Fast growing, evergreen with cone-
shaped crown. Bark peels to show
cream patches. Adult leaves
are lance-shaped and
curved, blue-green, 10–18 x 1.2–3 cm. Juvenile leaves are oval or rounded.
FLOWERS/FRUIT  Umbels of three flowers. Fruit is like a hemisphere,
5–8 x 7–9 mm.
HABITAT  Native to Tasmania, but also Victoria and New South Wales in
Australia. Grown as an ornamental tree throughout Europe.

## Cider gum
*Eucalyptus gunnii*

DESCRIPTION Height 20–30 m; bole up to 1 m diameter. Evergreen, with domed crown in mature trees. Bark peels in big flakes showing paler patches, which change to grey. Leaves come in two shapes – young are rounded or oval, green or blue-green, opposite; adult leaves are alternate, long and green, 6–10 x 3–4 cm.

FLOWERS/FRUIT Flowers in groups of three. Fruit is egg-shaped, ripens in summer with new flowers.

HABITAT Southern Australia and Tasmania. Mountainous forest. Grown as an ornamental tree and for forestry.

## Red gum
*Eucalyptus camuldulensis*

DESCRIPTION Height 20–80 m; bole up to 80 cm diameter. Evergreen. A broad, spreading crown with pendulous branchlets. Bark is flaky, showing patches of yellow or grey. Two kinds of leaves; juvenile leaves are lance-shaped, bluish; adult leaves are narrow, lance-shaped and curved, glaucous to pale green, 6–15 x 1– 2.5 cm.

FLOWERS/FRUIT Umbels consist of five to ten flowers. Fruit is like a hemisphere, 5–6 x 6–8 mm.

HABITAT Native to Australia. Widely grown for timber in temperate areas across Europe. Also ornamental.

## Tasmanian blue gum
### *Eucalyptus globulus*
DESCRIPTION Height 10–45 m; bole up to
2 m diameter. Evergreen. Crown is cone-
shaped at first, maturing into a tall dome.
The bark peels to reveal white, which
eventually becomes grey-brown. Juvenile
leaves are lance-shaped to oval, glaucous;
adult leaves are lance-shaped and curved,
leathery, blue-green, 10–30 x 3–4 cm. This is a
fast-growing tree, used for timber.
FLOWERS/FRUIT Single flowers are formed. Fruit
is globe-shaped, warty.
HABITAT Mainly Tasmania, but also native to Victoria,
Australia. Grown as an ornamental tree and for timber.

## Pomegranate
### *Punica granatus*
DESCRIPTION Height up to 8 m; bole up to
30 cm diameter. Deciduous. Crown is
rounded. Bark is brown, peeling off to show
whitish or buff beneath. Oval, narrow
leaves, 3.5–7 x 1–2.5 cm.
FLOWERS/FRUIT Bright red flowers occur singly
or in small groups, on this season's growth from
June onwards. Fruit is globe-shaped, with hard rind
and the calyx remains attached. It contains many,
semi-transparent pink seeds. Edible and good.
HABITAT Native to south-west Asia. Widely cultivated
in Mediterranean and other warm temperate areas.

### Dogwood
*Cornus sanguinea*

DESCRIPTION  Height 6 m, bole to 20 cm diameter. Crown is rounded. Bark is brown. The oval leaves are dark green, 4–8 x 2–4 cm. Autumn colour is red or purple. The blood-red shoots give this species its latin name "*sanguinea*".

FLOWERS/FRUIT  Fragrant, dull white flowers appear in June. Fruit is globe-shaped, turning from green to almost black, 6–8 mm, with a single seed.

HABITAT  Southern Scandinavia, Britain, Portugal, across Europe to Turkey. Understorey in woodlands.

### Pacific dogwood
*Cornus nuttallii*

DESCRIPTION  Height 15 m. Conical in shape. Deciduous. Leaves are oval, mid to dark green, 12 cm long. Red autumn colour.

FLOWERS/FRUIT  Flowers in late spring. Four to six, sometimes eight, large white bracts surround purple and green flowers. Flowerheads 1.5 cm. Fruits are spherical, orange-red.

HABITAT  Western North America. Prefers well-drained, neutral to acid soils.

## Oleaster
*Eleagnus angustifolia*
DESCRIPTION  Also known as Russian olive.
Height 6–12 m with rounded crown and
fissured bark. Leaves are lance-shaped,
underside silvered, 2.5–9 x 1–1.5 cm.
FLOWERS/FRUIT  Flowers in June, with fragrant
flowers that occur singly or sometimes in
groups of two or three. The oval-shaped fruit
is edible and ripens to yellow, 1–1.5 cm.
HABITAT  Native to Asia. Naturalised in
southern and central Europe. Grows on
open sites.

## Sea buckthorn
*Hippophae rhamnoides*
DESCRIPTION  Height 13 m, bole up to 30 cm
diameter. Deciduous. Grows as either a shrub
or small tree. Suckers grow from roots. Bark
is ridged, brown in colour. Leaves are
slender, silver-grey, 2.5–7.5 x 3–7 mm.
FLOWERS/FRUIT  Flowers in April, on
separate male and female trees. Fruit on
female plants are orange berries, holding
a single seed.
HABITAT  Western Europe, including Britain,
across to Asia and West China. Coastal
dunes and sandy areas.

## Spindle

*Euonymus europaeas*

DESCRIPTION Height 6–10 m, bole up to 25 cm diameter. Deciduous. Crown
is egg-shaped, branches are ascending. Bark is fissured, grey-brown in colour.
Leaves are elliptical, tapering, turning pink-red in autumn, 2.5–8 x 1–3 cm.
FLOWERS/FRUIT Three to five yellow-green flowers are borne in May to June.
The fruits have four lobes, are pendent, pink-red, 1.2–1.5 cm.
HABITAT Native to most of Europe, but not the extreme south or north.
Woodland, hedgerows and scrub. Likes chalk and lime soils. Wood from
this tree was used to make spindles.

# Holly

*Ilex aquifolium*

DESCRIPTION  Height to 10–25 m, bole up to 1m diameter.
Evergreen. Narrow-crowned conical tree. Bark green when
young, smooth and grey later. Leaves are alternate with
sharp spines, dark green glossy on top, pale green beneath
and hairless, 5–12 x 2–6 cm. Leaves tend to become
smoother, less spiky, as tree ages, especially
near top of crown, just retaining end point.

FLOWERS/FRUIT  Male and female flowers
appear in May on separate trees.
Pollinated by insects. Only female
trees bear berries.

HABITAT  Native to western
Europe to western Asia. Many
cultivars – popular as
ornamental garden trees and
for hedging. Woodland and
hedgerows. Leaves were used
as winter feed for livestock; the
wood was used to make whips.

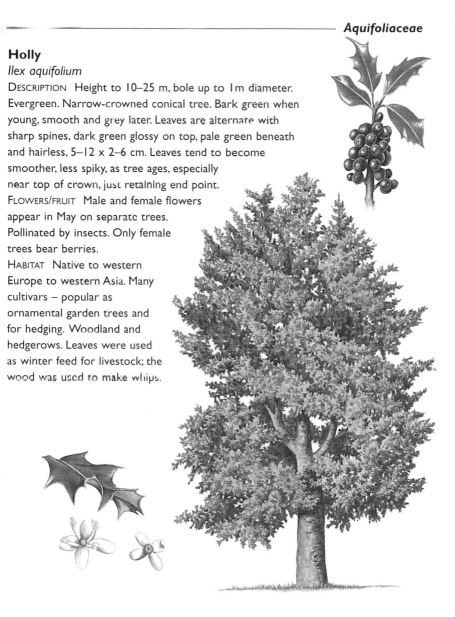

## Box

*Buxus sempervirens*

DESCRIPTION Height 6 m, bole up to 30 cm diameter. Evergreen. A spreading shrub or narrow tree. Bark is pale brown, cracking into squares. Leaves opposite in sprays, oval, mid to dark green, 1.2–2.5 x 0.5–1.1 cm. Timber is high quality.

FLOWERS/FRUIT Clusters of five to eight male flowers and one female flower at the end are produced in late spring. The fruit is almost globe-shaped, blue-green, 7 mm. Seeds are black and shiny.

HABITAT Central and southern Europe. Widely planted as hedging shrub, especially in formal gardens. Prefers brick soils, on dry hills. Can withstand dense shade.

## Purging buckthorn
*Rhamnus catharticus*

DESCRIPTION Height 6 m. Deciduous. Large shrub to small tree with rounded crown and brown bark. Leaves are elliptic, dull green, 2.5–7 x 1.2–3.5 cm.

FLOWERS/FRUIT Flowers are unobtrusive yellow-green. The fruit is almost globe-shaped, purple-black, 6 mm, and gives the tree its purgative qualities.

HABITAT Native to Europe and north Asia. Found on sandy scrub and chalk downland.

## Alder buckthorn
*Frangula alnus*

DESCRIPTION Height 6 m, bole up to 20 cm diameter. Deciduous shrub or small tree with rounded crown with several stems and bark that is dark-brown, showing yellow beneath if cut. Leaves are oval, tapered, with wavy margins, 3–7 x 2.5–4 cm.

FLOWERS/FRUIT Small clusters. Flowers are formed in leaf axils. Fruit is globe-shaped, ripening to purple, 6–10 mm.

HABITAT Central and northern Europe, including Britain. Hedgerows and understorey in moist woodland.

## Horse chestnut
*Aesculus hippocastanum*

DESCRIPTION Height to 20–35 m, bole up to 2.2 m diameter. Deciduous. Crown is domed. Bark is red-brown or dark grey-brown and scaly. Branches are arching, usually turned up at the end. Leaves have five to seven large stalkless, leaflets, broader towards tip, 13–30 x 2–13 cm.

FLOWERS/FRUIT Flowers are showy white panicles on spikes opening in May, 20–30 cm. The globe-shaped spiny fruit contains one or more large shiny brown nuts (conkers), 3–5 cm.

HABITAT Native to the Balkan peninsula. Planted as an ornamental elsewhere. Mixed woodland, parks.

## Field maple
*Acer campestris*

DESCRIPTION Height 10–12 m, occasionally to 28 m. Deciduous. Has rounded dome and grey-brown scaly bark that darkens in old trees. Leaves have five lobes, 7 x 7 cm, may be pink or purplish when new, turning yellow in autumn. Produces good quality timber.

FLOWERS/FRUIT Flowers are not very obvious but appear after leaves. The fruit is flat on a pair of wings, 2.5–5 cm.

HABITAT Central to southern Europe, including England and Wales. Deciduous, broadleaf woodlands. Hedgerows. Will grow in sandy, chalk or clay soils.

# Sycamore

*Acer pseudoplatanus*

DESCRIPTION Height 15–35 m, bole up to 2 m. Deciduous. Massive domed crown in mature trees. Bark is grey and smooth, becoming scaly and fissured. Leaves have five pointed lobes, the lower lobes are not fully separated, dark green on top, pale underneath, 10–20 x 10–20 cm.

FLOWERS/FRUIT Flowers appear in April to June, in a dense panicle hanging like catkins. Fruit is hairless with wings at 50–60° angle, 2.5–3 x 0.8–1 cm. Two single seeds dispersed by wing.

HABITAT Western Europe, east to Caucasus and Crimea. Naturalized elsewhere. Woodland and forests.

## Norway maple
*Acer platanoides*

DESCRIPTION Height 15–25 m, bole up to 1.3 m diameter. Deciduous. Young trees have egg-shaped crown that becomes rounded or dome-shaped. Bark is smooth, developing shallow fissures. Leaves have five lobes, new leaves may be purplish, turning yellow in autumn, 7–14 x 8–20 cm.

FLOWERS/FRUIT Flowers are usually yellow-green, in early spring before leaves emerge. The fruit is a flat nut with wings.

HABITAT Europe from southern Sweden and southern Norway to Crimea. Widely planted, especially as an amenity tree in towns. Woodland.

## Black walnut
*Juglans nigra*

DESCRIPTION Height 15–35 m, bole up to 2 m diameter. Deciduous. Crown is domed or rounded. The bark is usually dark brown, deeply furrowed and ridged. Leaves are large, 30–60 cm, with 9–23 lance-shaped, tapered leaflets.

FLOWERS/FRUIT Small green flowers appear in spring, with yellow male catkins. The fruit is smooth with a thick fleshy covering over a large nut, 3–5 cm. Edible and good.

HABITAT Native to North America. Also grown as an ornamental tree elsewhere. Prefers streamside sites. The husk can be used to make a dark dye.

**Walnut**
*Juglans regia*
DESCRIPTION Height
15–25 m, bole up to 2 m
diameter. Deciduous. Crown is
rounded and branches
radiating. Bark is
smooth, shiny and grey at first, becoming ridged, with wide fissures.
Leaves are pinnate, with five to nine oval leaflets, 20 x 10 cm.
FLOWERS/FRUIT Male catkins are 5–10 cm long and appear at the end of new
shoots. Female catkins in clusters on old wood. Globe-shaped fruits have
a thick green fleshy case, splitting to reveal a large nut, 4–5 cm. The nut has
an excellent flavour. Squirrels and large birds such as rooks also eat them.
HABITAT South-east Europe to central Asia across to China. Widely
cultivated. Woodland.

## Olive
*Olea europaea*
DESCRIPTION Height to 15 m, bole up to 1 m diameter. Evergreen. The trunk is short, with rounded, spreading crown and silver-grey bark. Leaves are lance-shaped, grey-green, whitish below, 2–8 x 0.8–2 cm.

FLOWERS/FRUIT Flowers on current season's growth in July to August. The flowers are fragrant and produced in panicles. The egg- or globe-shaped fruits take a year or so to ripen from green to brown or black, 1–3.5 cm. Edible and good.
HABITAT Grown throughout the Mediterranean region. Hillsides.

## Narrow-leafed ash
*Fraxinus angustifolia*
DESCRIPTION Height to 15–30 m, bole up to 1.1 m diameter. Deciduous. This tree has an irregular, domed crown, with branches that curve upwards. The bark is grey with deep fissures and growing bumps as the tree ages. Leaves are pinnate, with 7–13 pairs of leaflets; lance-shaped, tapered, 3–9 x 0.8–2 cm.
FLOWERS/FRUIT Flowers are small, petal-less and appear before the leaves. The fruit is a winged nutlet, 2–4.5 cm, green maturing to brown.
HABITAT Western Mediterranean. Near rivers. Deciduous woodland.

## Ash

*Fraxinus excelsior*

DESCRIPTION  Height 20–30 m, bole up to 1 m diameter. Deciduous. Upper branches are ascending, lower ones curve downwards sometimes almost vertically, then turn upwards near the tip. Bark is green-grey and fissures with age. Leaves are pinnate, 20–35 cm with 9–13 stalked, toothed leaflets.

FLOWERS/FRUIT  Male and female flowers occur on the same tree on separate twigs in purplish clusters during April and May. Fruits are long seed pods that hang down in dense clusters. Winged seeds are called "keys".

HABITAT  Europe east to the Caucasus. Woodland, forest, hedgerows. Valuable timber tree, its white wood was used to make carriage shafts.

## Manna ash
*Fraxinus ornus*

DESCRIPTION Height 15–25 m, bole up to 1 m diameter. Deciduous. This tree usually has a rounded crown with spreading branches. The bark is dark grey, smooth. The leaves are pinnate, 20–30 cm total length, comprising five to nine leaflets that are variable in shape.

FLOWERS/FRUIT Flowers differ markedly from *F. excelsior*. They are white to creamy, in 20 cm panicles, appearing in May. Fruit is a winged nutlet, 1.5–2.5 cm.

HABITAT Southern Europe through to Asia Minor.

## Privet
*Ligustrum vulgare*

DESCRIPTION Straggling shrub, height to 5 m. Evergreen, but some leaves fall in cold weather. Branches are long, arching over and rooting where they make contact with soil, making thickets. Leaves are lance-shaped, opposite, 2–10 x 1–5 cm, on short stalks.

FLOWERS/FRUIT Flowers appear in June to July, white in terminal panicles, 5–10 x 5–10 cm. Fruit is a purple-black, poisonous berry, 7–8 mm, containing 2–4 seeds, ripening September.

HABITAT Widespread throughout Europe. Widely used as a hedging shrub. Prefers lime and chalk soils.

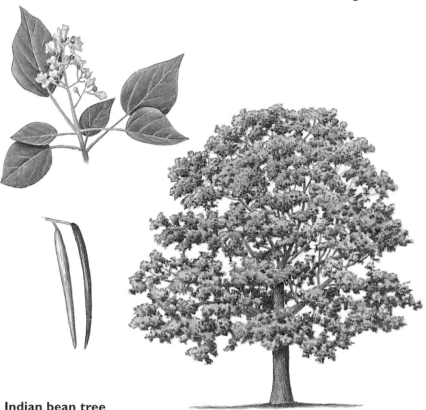

## Indian bean tree

*Catalpa bignonioides*

DESCRIPTION  Height 10–15 m, bole up to 1.1 m diameter. Deciduous. Bark is smooth, pink and brown in young trees, becoming grey and scaly with plates. The leaves are egg-shaped, with a slender, pointed tip, 12–25 x 10–18 cm.

FLOWERS/FRUIT  Flowers are showy, with tube-shaped white petals with red and purple inner markings, in panicles of 20–30 cm. The fruit, containing many winged seeds, is a purple pod, 15–40 cm.

HABITAT  Native to southern states of North America. Widely grown as an ornamental tree. Woodland edges.

## Elder
*Sambucus nigra*
DESCRIPTION Height 10 m, bole up to 50 cm diameter. Deciduous. Crown is rounded. Bark is light brown, or grey, thick, deeply fissured and corky. Many branches arise from base, later arch back towards the ground. Leaves are opposite, with terminal leaflet, two or three pairs of lateral leaflets, 3–9 cm.

FLOWERS/FRUIT Flowers are creamy-white, 5 mm across, massed in large clusters with flat-topped head and a heavy, sweet scent. Purple berries ripening in August and September.

HABITAT Widespread through Europe, North Africa. Common in hedgerows.

## Wayfaring tree
*Viburnum lantana*
DESCRIPTION Height 6 m. Deciduous shrub with spreading habit; rounded, bushy crown. Bark is brown. Leaves are heart-shaped at base, opposite and sharply toothed with white hairs underneath, 5–12 x 3–10 cm.

FLOWERS/FRUIT Flowers in May and June. Flowers are all alike and fertile, forming a dense, cream-coloured dome. Fruit is a red, oval berry, produced in July to September, turning to black with maturity, 8 mm.

HABITAT Southern and central Europe to North Africa. Hedgerows, verges.

## Guelder rose
*Viburnum opulus*

DESCRIPTION  Height 6 m. Deciduous. Spreading shrub with few branches. Leaves are opposite with three to five lobes, smooth and hairless on upper surface, hairy beneath, 5–10 cm. Leaves turn red in autumn.

FLOWERS/FRUIT  Dense heads of small, white, fertile flowers, surrounded by bigger, showy, sterile flowers, 15–20 mm across in June and July. Fruits are round, ripening to transparent red in September to October, hanging in clusters.

HABITAT  Europe to central Asia and North Africa. Hedgerows and woodland.

# Addresses

Plantlife
21 Elizabeth Street
London SW1W 9RP
Tel  020 7808 0100
Fax  020 7730 8377
E-mail  enquiries@plantlife.org.uk
Website  www.plantlife.org.uk

Tree Advice Trust
Alice Holt Lodge
Farnham
Surrey GU10 4LH
Tel  01420 22022
Fax  01420 22000
Advice helpline 09065 161147
E-mail  admin@treeadviceservice.org.uk
Website  www.treeadviceservice.org.uk

The Wildlife Trusts
The Kiln
Waterside
Mather Road
Newark
Nottinghamshire NG24 1WT
Tel  0870 036 7711
Fax  0870 036 0101
E-mail  info@wildlife-trusts.cix.co.uk
Website  www.wildlifetrusts.org

Wildlife Watch
(Contact details as above)
E-mail  watch@wildlifetrusts.cix.co.uk

# Suggested reading

Coombes, Allen J.
*Trees*
Dorling Kindersley, 1992

Gibbons, Bob & Brough, Peter
*The Hamlyn Photographic Guide to the Wild
Flowers of Britain & Northern Europe*
Hamlyn, 1992

Mitchell, Alan
*A Field Guide to the Trees of Britain and
Northern Europe*
Collins, 1974

Rackham, Oliver
*The Illustrated History of the Countryside*
Weidenfield & Nicholson, 1994

Rose, Francis
*The Wild Flower Key*
Warne, 1981

Rushforth, Keith
*Trees of Britain and Europe*
HarperCollins, 1999

# Index

## Common names

## Scientific names